AMERICAN HISTORY

IN VERSE

583 2514

Copyright © 1976, by John Van Duyn Southworth

All rights reserved. No part of this book may be used or reproduced in any manner without written permission except in the case of excerpts or brief quotations embodied in articles and reviews. For information address Valkyrie Press, Inc., 2135 1st Avenue South, St. Petersburg, Florida 33712.

First Edition
ISBN: 0-912760-20-6
Library of Congress Catalog Card Number: 76-590

PUBLISHED BY

ST. PETERSBURG, FLORIDA

Dedication

To my dear friend,

Marjorie Massey Schuck

Other publications by
John Van Duyn Southworth

HOW TO STUDY
OUR OWN UNITED STATES
THE STORY OF THE WORLD
THE PIRATE FROM ROME
MONARCH AND CONSPIRATORS

THE WAR AT SEA SERIES:
1. THE ANCIENT FLEETS
2. THE AGE OF SAILS
3. THE AGE OF STEAM, PART ONE
4. THE AGE OF STEAM, PART TWO

THE IROQUOIS TIME LINE FOR ALL HISTORY
THE AMERICAN HISTORY TIME LINE AND DATE CHART
THE WORLD CIVILIZATION TIME LINE

plus seventeen other books, mostly histories,
in co-authorship with other writers.

TABLE OF CONTENTS

PAGE No.

Preface	11
The Indian	15
Christopher Columbus	16
The Pilgrims	17
Pilgrims and Indians	18
John Harvard	21
Torquemada and Cotton Mather	22
Isaac Jogues and Jean Lalande	23
"Mother Goose"	25
William Dawes and Samuel Prescott	27
George Washington	29
Betsy Ross	31
The Signers	32
Patrick Henry	35
Thomas Paine	38
"Mad Anthony" Wayne	40
Daniel Boone	41
Alexander Hamilton	43
Mystery Lady	45
"John Paul Jones"	47
"Molly Pitcher"	49
Benedict Arnold	50
The Rivals — John Adams and Thomas Jefferson	52
Benjamin Franklin	55
James Madison	57
Eli Whitney	59
The Whisky Rebellion	61
John James Audubon	63
Aaron Burr	64
Andrew Jackson	65

	PAGE No.
Francis Scott Key	69
Henry Clay	71
Donald McKay	73
Stephen Foster	75
Stephen Douglas	76
Ulysses S. Grant and Robert E. Lee	77
David Farragut	79
Abraham Lincoln	81
Street Incident	82
The Gun-Slingers	83
Alexander Graham Bell	84
Henry Ford	87
George Washington Carver	88
The Wright Brothers	91
Carry Nation	92
The Suffragettes	93
Phineas T. Barnum	95
Man of Contradictions	96
Vermont Does Not Answer	97
Lee De Forest	98
Grandma Moses	99
Franklin Delano Roosevelt	101
Parker Buck — Neighborhood Hero	103
Ralph Bunche, Pioneer	105
"We" — Charles Augustus Lindbergh	107
To A U.N. Soldier Dead in a Distant Land	108
Presidential Jinx	113
The Unknown Future	115
Index	118

LIST OF ILLUSTRATIONS

	PAGE NO.
The Indian	14
"Mother Goose"	24
"The British Are Coming"	26
George Washington	28
Betsy Ross	30
Patrick Henry	34
Alexander Hamilton	42
"John Paul Jones"	46
"Molly Pitcher"	48
Benjamin Franklin	54
John James Audubon	62
Francis Scott Key	68
Abraham Lincoln	80
Henry Ford	86
The Wright Brothers	90
Phineas T. Barnum	94
Franklin Delano Roosevelt	100
Ralph Bunche, Pioneer	104
Presidential Jinx	112
The Unknown Future	117

THE AMERICANA COLLECTION
of
Ron Reams

THE INDIAN — *The Voice of Man*

ABRAHAM LINCOLN — *As I Would Not Be A Slave*

THE WRIGHT BROTHERS — *The Air Age Had Arrived*

HENRY FORD — *He Who Would Really Benefit Mankind Must Reach Them Through His Work.*

FRANKLIN DELANO ROOSEVELT — *The Only Thing We Have To Fear Is Fear Itself.*

JOHN F. KENNEDY — *And We Are All Mortal.*

— PREFACE —

Why in the world would one undertake to express the facts and personalities of history in verse? Why, indeed?

One truthful answer must surely be, "Why, just for the Hell of it!"

When one loves history, enjoys to the full reading exceptional presentations of this or that event, the temptation is strong to try to add an unusual presentation of one's own. This was one of the inspirations which lay behind the writing of my texts in history and it also added incentive to the writing of these verses.

Verse-writing has enchantments of its own. One who enjoys the handling of language gets real pleasure from the searching out of the precisely-needed rhyme, the phrasing and rephrasing of this line or that to achieve the exact effect desired, and even the perpetration of the occasional and probably inexcusable pun. The writing of verse opens the door to enjoyment of this sort.

The following collection had its genesis long years ago when I was a teacher of history. Students all too often lose sight of the concept worth retaining, permitting it to become obscured and lost in a forest of verbiage and detail. An occasional epigram — quoted or home-grown — helped meet this situation. So did an occasional verse, written sharply to the point. Some of the earliest of these little "poems" had their origin in this.

In 1960, when a heart attack had forced me to curtail my activities, I gathered together some of my historical verses and sent them to *Grit* — the amazing country weekly with a circulation of well over a million. *Grit* liked them, published them, and asked for more. The result was a regular feature, "History in Verse," running from mid-1960 well into 1962. A good many of the verses in this book were written for that special series. They are here reproduced with the magazine's permission and are listed on the following page.

No pretense is made that this book contains great poetry, as the readers will discover for themselves. Most of the selections are not, in fact, poetry at all. They are rhymes, jingles, doggerel, verse   and sometimes worse. A few are in free verse. These and a very few others are serious. All in all, the selections represent a most surprising synthesis of the author's serious work as an historian and the type of light verse he used to write for the pages of the Harvard *Lampoon*.

Nuf sed! I hope that several of these poems, at least, will give the reader pleasure in some way comparable to that which I experienced in framing them.

— John Van Duyn Southworth

The following poems are reproduced with kind permission of *Grit* magazine.

STEPHEN FOSTER	HENRY FORD	THE WRIGHT BROTHERS
THOMAS PAINE	GRANDMA MOSES	STEPHEN DOUGLAS
COLUMBUS	DAVID FARRAGUT	LEE DeFOREST
THE GUN-SLINGERS	JOHN HARVARD	AARON BURR
MOTHER GOOSE	THE INDIAN	JOHN JAMES AUDUBON
DONALD McKAY	JOHN PAUL	GEORGE WASHINGTON
CARRY NATION	MAD ANTHONY WAYNE	Wm. DAWES AND SAMUEL PRESCOTT
ALEXANDER GRAHAM BELL	MOLLY PITCHER	THE WHISKY REBELLION
	THE PILGRIMS	

AMERICAN HISTORY

IN VERSE

By John Van Duyn Southworth

ILLUSTRATED By Ronald D. Reams

Valkyrie Press, Inc.

THE INDIAN

Lo, the poor Indian,
    Stalking the woods,
Building no cities,
    Making no goods,

Hunting and fishing,
    Fighting a bit,
Disdaining all labor —
    Preferring to sit,

Bestirring himself
    But for hunting and wars,
Letting his squaw
    Perform all the chores.

How could the white man,
    In ignorant bliss,
Think he could better
    A system like this?

CHRISTOPHER COLUMBUS
(1451-1506 A.D.)

Far off to the westward
    Stretched the ocean wide.
Strongly at your moorings
    Pulled the flowing tide.
You would sail out westward
    With a dream for guide.

        You were sure, Columbus,
            Certain all along,
        You would sail to Asia.
            You were wrong!

High above the island
    Blazed the tropic sky.
Palm trees fringed the beaches.
    Mountains towered high.
There you dropped your anchors,
    Safe at rest to lie.

        You were sure, Columbus,
            Certain all along,
        You had reached far Asia.
            You were wrong!

Back at home in Europe,
    In the court of Spain,
You revealed your treasures,
    Brought across the main,
Told of your adventures
    In the far terrain.

        You were sure, Columbus,
            Certain all along,
        You had been to Asia.
            You were wrong!

THE PILGRIMS

(c. 1620 A.D.)

For daring to defy King James
    And cross the stormy sea,
For working, starving, building homes
    In a savage, cold country,
For braving beasts and Indians,
    Enduring anguished days —
For all these things we freely give
    The Pilgrim Fathers praise.

But wait a minute! Shouldn't we
    Bestow this praise on others?
Should we not give a greater share
    Unto the Pilgrim Mothers?
Just like the men, they too endured
    Those perils, toils, and bothers,
And, worst of all, they had to face
    Those same stern Pilgrim Fathers!

PILGRIMS AND INDIANS

The Pilgrims had landed, and Plymouth was there,
    Its roots groping down through the soil.
It seemed that the settlement might well succeed,
    At the cost of much unceasing toil.

One item of danger remained very real
    And caused many Pilgrims to fret.
Would the copper-skinned natives accept the new town,
    Or were they a dangerous threat?

One day, from the forest, a warrior strode
    And marched up the single, wide street.
In fear and in hope, the Pilgrims came forth
    To listen, oppose, or to greet.

Though no Pilgrims knew it, the Indian brave
    Had a talent no others could boast.
Alone of his people, he'd learned English speech
    From some fishermen met on the coast.

He gazed at their faces, did brave Samoset,
    Causing fear, causing worry, and then
At last he delivered his message of fate:
    "Welcome," he exclaimed, "Englishmen!"

Not many weeks later, the tribesman returned,
    Bringing with him a brave of renown.
This Indian, Squanto, was anxious to stay —
    To settle and live in the town.

The Pilgrims were happy to welcome him there,
    For he taught them the things they should know
To live in an unsettled wilderness land
    That had never felt mattock or hoe.

In the wake of the two helpful braves from the tribe,
    Another, much greater, appeared.
Chief Massasoit came, and with him he brought
    Sixty warriors, as many had feared.

Squanto warned of their coming; the townsfolk turned out
    Each man with a drum or a gun.
Each group was impressed by the other's array,
    And no hostile actions were done.

By the end of the meeting, firm friendships replaced
    The early suspicions and fears.
A treaty was signed, which led to a peace
    Which was honored for fifty long years.

Chief Canonicus headed another tribe there.
    Plymouth looked to him easy to take.
As a symbol of war he sent arrows galore
    Bound up in the skin of a snake.

Miles Standish knew how to answer a threat.
    The snake skin was quickly sent back,
Filled full of gunpowder and bullets this time.
    The chief never made his attack.

JOHN HARVARD
(1607-1638 A.D.)

When to our wilderness you came
    In sixteen thirty-seven
You found that Massachusetts Bay
    Was not a bit like Heaven.

The woods were thick, the buildings few,
    In what would be our nation.
Some farms there were, some churches, too,
    But little education.

And yet, in Cambridge, certain men
    Of vision, skill, and knowledge
Were trying to emplant a school
    That might become a college.

You saw, approved, and in your will,
    To help them educate,
You left them every book you owned
    And half of your estate.

Next year, you died at thirty-one.
    Your relatives all grieved.
The educators hailed with joy
    The gift they had received.

The passing centuries have seen
    Far greater gifts, it's true,
But none that's won the same acclaim.
    They named the school for you!

Ah, many wealthy Harvard men
    Would give their gold in mounds
For what you got for certain books
    And seven-eighty pounds!

NOTE: This poem contains a flagrant example of "poetic license." John Harvard's cash bequest was not "seven-eighty pounds" but seven hundred seventy-nine pounds, seventeen shillings, twopence. The author is happy to announce that he has lately sent to Harvard University the princely sum of 29¢, to be credited to the bequest of the Reverend John Harvard, thus squaring the account and preserving the meter.

TORQUEMADA AND COTTON MATHER*

(1420-1498; 1663-1728 A.D.)

In the deepest, hottest pit of Hell
You two will sizzle mighty well!

Although your holy doctrines varied,
An equal load of guilt you carried.
You sentenced the heretic, *you* the witch,
To a slow and frightful punishment which
Condemned them to torture and pain and crying
Until released by the mercy of dying.

The Devil will greet you two as brothers
For forcing religious beliefs on others!

---

*Tomas de Torquemada was a harsh persecutor of heretics for the Catholic Church during the middle ages. Cotton Mather, a Massachusetts Puritan, was known as a cruel persecutor of witches — to him, another form of heretic, or unbeliever.

ISAAC JOGUES AND JEAN LALANDE

(d. 1646 A.D.)

From France you came to the New World
    To spread the word of God —
Two Jesuits to preach and pray
    Where saints had never trod.

With faith undimmed, you carried out
    The mission you'd received,
Until at last you found yourselves
    Both captured and deceived.

The Mohawk tribesmen would not hear
    The message you had brought.
To them, you were two enemies
    To die as soon as caught.

You died in pain, as martyrs do,
    Your names and faiths untainted.
Almost three centuries would pass
    Before you would be sainted.

This was, it seems, a long delay,
    Redressing your sad fate.
All we can do is to admit
    Your canons came too late.

NOTE: This is admittedly a bad pun. Most readers, but not all, will know that a canon is an order or ruling issued by the Roman Catholic Church and approved by the Pope.

"MOTHER GOOSE"

(Elizabeth Vergoose, c. 1685 A.D.)

When at your knee you gathered up
    The Boston girls and boys,
Your verses spun a magic web.
    Their hearts were filled with joys
Which led them to forget that they
    Could have few games or toys.

Your wondrous world of common things
    Enchanted little folks
Who could enjoy, in simple verse,
    Uncomplicated jokes.
They rallied round most eagerly.
    You never had to coax.

All honor to you, Mother Goose!
    You knew how children feel.
For centuries, fond mothers have
    Retold your verse with zeal.
Too bad so many of them now
    Forget that you were real!

WILLIAM DAWES AND SAMUEL PRESCOTT

(1745-1799; 1751-1777 A.D.)

Three men rode through the moonlight clear
    With hoofbeats madly drumming.
Cried Prescott, Dawes, and Paul Revere,
    "The regulars are coming!"

Both Dawes and Prescott reached their goal
    And spread the word of warning.
Revere was caught by a patrol
    And held until the morning.

All three deserved a hero's name.
    It was most unexpected
That only one lived on in fame;
    The others were neglected.

Why such injustice? What's the cause?
    Just think, and you will know it.
What rhymes with Prescott or with Dawes
    That would attract a poet?

Revere has had his story told.
    It's frequently recited.
Now to the light we must uphold
    The two who have been slighted.

GEORGE WASHINGTON
(1732-1799 A.D.)

A tricorn hat, a cherry bunch,
    A hatchet bright and new —
Are these the things we should recall
    When thinking, sir, of you?
Or should we think of courage which
    Could see a lost cause through?

Should we, like prissy Parson Weems,
    Insist you could not lie?
Deception was your stock in trade
    When British troops were nigh.
At Trenton and at Princeton you
    Deceived them — made them fly.

Should we recall your powdered wigs,
    Your uniforms so trim,
Or should our inner eye behold
    A visage sad and grim —
A man who knew his foe was strong
    But would not yield to him?

Should we complacently recall
    The honors you received,
Or think of angry insults and
    A patient soul aggrieved?
Few men have been so blamed as you
    For honest gains achieved.

Our symbolism does you wrong —
    The cherries, hatchet, hat;
The prim and righteous little boy,
    So good, so true, so *flat*!
We look again and see you were
    A greater man than that.

BETSY ROSS

(1752-1836 A.D.)

Oh, Betsy Ross, of Quaker Town,
   Is the old story true?
Did you sew stripes of red and white
   And thirteen stars on blue?
Was our first flag the product of
   Your needle, thread, and you?

Historians, who deal in facts,
   Seem anxious to be rid
Of all the tales that can't be proved.
   Your story they forbid.
But, as for me, I much prefer
   To think you really did.

THE SIGNERS

(July 4, 1776)

What a wonderful chance to be noted!
   What a marvelous thing for your fame!
What man wouldn't long for such glory,
   To be had just by signing his name?

The fifty-six members of Congress
   All signed that they wished to be free,
Endorsing our land's independence
   From the Motherland, over the sea.

Lucky men, putting pen to the paper
   That would add them to history's list!
Would *you* have stepped forward and signed it?
   Of course! It's no chance to be missed!

Think a little. In signing that paper,
    They were betting their lives on a hope,
Defying a mighty world power
    That might end their lives with a rope.

They were brave men, but were they immortal?
    How great was their actual fame?
Of the fifty-six men who were signers,
    How many, off hand, can *you* name?

NOTE: It's a rare person, indeed, who can name half-a-dozen of the signers of the Declaration of Independence. Most lead off with Thomas Jefferson, who had written the Declaration and of course signed it, and John Hancock, who started the signing by writing his name "large enough for King George to read without his spectacles." John Adams, Samuel Adams, and Benjamin Franklin are good and accurate guesses. Then whom do you name? The other signers were Roger Sherman, Samuel Huntington, William Williams, Oliver Wolcott, Caesar Rodney, George Read, Thomas McKean, Button Gwinnett, Lyman Hall, George Walton, Samuel Chase, William Paca, Thomas Stone, Charles Carroll, Robert Treat Paine, Elbridge Gerry,. Josiah Bartlett, William Whipple, Matthew Thornton, Richard Stockton, John Witherspoon, Francis Hopkinson, John Hart, Abraham Clark, William Floyd, Philip Livingston, Francis Lewis, Lewis Morris, William Hooper, Joseph Hewes, John Penn, Robert Morris, Benjamin Rush, John Morton, George Clymer, James Smith, George Taylor, James Wilson, George Ross, Stephen Hopkins, William Ellery, Edward Rutledge, Thomas Heyward, Jr., Thomas Lynch, Jr., Arthur Middleton, George Wythe, Richard Henry Lee, Benjamin Harrison, Thomas Nelson, Jr., Francis Lightfoot Lee, and Carter Braxton – the entire membership of the Second Continental Congress.

PATRICK HENRY

(1737-1799 A.D.)

We know you, Patrick Henry,
Not for great personal success
(For you had little)
But for your iron nerve,
Your fluent tongue,
Marshaling our language,
Sending it out to fight and win
In vital causes.

When George III, King of England,
Who thought the colonies were his to loot,
Forced the Stamp Act through his Parliament,
Most of the colonists feared to object.
They feared, that is,
Until they heard of your bold defiance,
Voiced in Virginia's House of Burgesses:
"Caesar had his Brutus;
Charles the First his Cromwell;
And George the Third . . . "
(Cries of "Treason! Treason!")
". . . May profit from their example. . .
If this be treason, make the most of it."

Your message spread.
Throughout the colonies a new message was voiced:
"Taxation without representation is tyranny."
The stamp men were resisted,
British goods boycotted,
King George's Stamp Act repealed.

No final victory had been achieved.
The British King was making ready
To force his will upon the colonies.
"The King and Parliament
Have full power and authority
To bind the colonies and people of America
In all cases whatsoever."
So said the English Declaratory Act,
A warning of things to come.
As you and others knew,
Force must be met by force,
Arms checked by arms.
Again, your voice was heard:
"I know not what course others may take,
But, as for me,
Give me liberty or give me death."
The colonies armed themselves,
Stood together, and won their independence.

Were you of two minds, Patrick Henry,
Concerning constitutions?
You had helped to frame a new one for your state,
For Virginia,
But when a national constitution was drawn up
You opposed it.
Why?

The men chosen to draft this new government
Were from a single class,
The wealthy.
Their new government was too powerful,
Too slanted toward the upper class.
It protected their interests and their wealth
But offered little
For the common people and the states.
"Most awfully alarmed,"
You insisted on ten amendments,
A Bill of Rights,
To be added before the Constitution was approved.
These did much to make all classes even
Before their government.
Now, with clear conscience, you could favor
The new Constitution.
You did.
It was adopted.

You were still active
When your time ran out.
You had been offered high positions.
You had rejected all.
But when the people of Virginia chose you
For their legislature —
The same office you had held
When you started your rise to fame —
You cheerfully accepted.
You died, though,
Before you had a chance
To serve again.

We all owe much to you,
Patrick Henry.
It was your voice, your nerve,
Your skillful choice of words
That moved us to take action
When it was needed most.

THOMAS PAINE

(1737-1809 A.D.)

From England came poor Thomas Paine,
    To serve a cause which he
Could see was fraught with hopelessness —
    Our struggle to be free.

His keen, incisive mind and pen
    Revealed the very thing
That split America in two —
    Our war against a king

To whom we still pledged loyalty.
    He authored *Common Sense.*
Its logic was so clear and sharp
    We climbed down from the fence.

Our independence we declared.
    Then, when the war seemed lost,
Paine wrote *The Crisis*, urging men
    To fight, nor count the cost.

The war was won. Our land was free.
    Poor Tom could rest his brain.
Much credit went to Washington,
    Not much to Thomas Paine.

"Where Freedom is, there is my home,"
    Ben Franklin proudly cried.
"Where there's no Freedom, there I'll dwell,"
    Poor Thomas Paine replied.

Across the seas, in far-off France,
    There still was tyranny.
Tom saw a need for freedom there,
    So off once more went he.

Tom's been reviled, with epithets.
    He managed not to heed 'em.
But now we know him as the first
    True Citizen of Freedom.

"MAD ANTHONY" WAYNE

(1745-1796 A.D.)

Were you really insane,
"Mad Anthony" Wayne,
When you tried what no others would try?
Was it daring and pluck
Or just crazy luck
That led you to win, not to die?

When you crept through the night
Without glimmer of light,
Guns unloaded and bayonets fixed;
When you charged with a yell
And Fort Stony Point fell,
Were your mind and emotions all mixed?

When the Indians fled
From the troops that you led,
Were you acting as maniacs do?
Were you really insane,
"Mad Anthony" Wayne?
More men should be crazy like you!

DANIEL BOONE
(1734-1820 A.D.)

The Indians called it Kentucky —
    "The dark, bloody land," so they said —
They boasted that any white settlers
    Who went there would quickly be dead.

Things grew worse when another threat sounded,
    Throughout all the colonies heard:
"No settlers may go past the mountains,"
    Declared Britain's King, George the Third.

Who would dare to defy the fierce Redmen
    And the word of the King to impugn?
One man in the colonies tried it —
    A bold guide and leader, Dan Boone.

The chances he took were amazing.
    One learns, with a shortness of breath,
That he led many groups to Kentucky,
    Though frequently threatened with death.

From his fortified town in Kentucky,
    He fought with a veteran's lore
'gainst the Indian tribes and the British
    Through the years of our nation's first war.

One might think, with the risks Boone had taken,
    He'd relax and enjoy a long rest,
But we soon find him settling Missouri,
    Newly gained in our wide-open West.

The moral that goes with this story?
    There *is* one, without any doubt.
A really great man keeps achieving
    As long as his life-strength holds out.

ALEXANDER HAMILTON
(1755-1804 A.D.)

Bright boy, from Nevis in the Isles,
   Sharp writer at nineteen,
You soon became a brilliant man
   Whose like is seldom seen.

When trouble came with England's King
   You shouldered quite a weight.
Your pamphlets, speeches, arguments
   Did much to set us straight.

You weren't content with politics.
   Before the war was done,
You'd showed great courage in the field,
   Supporting Washington.

The Articles which held the states
   Together through the war
Were not enough. You made the call
   That got us something more.

The men who answered to your call
   From thirteen states were sent.
They got together and produced
   A stronger government.

The Fed'ralist, which now appeared,
   Did much to put it through.
Of all the brilliant arguments,
   Most had been penned by you.

With Washington as President
    And you to run finance,
This government gave ample sign
    Of having every chance.

It stayed alive, it gained in strength,
    It would not be denied,
And some new powers it assumed
    Had been, you said, "implied."

Although you left the government
    For law in ninety-five,
You kept on writing, urging things,
    To make the country thrive.

One dreadful error was that duel
    You fought with Aaron Burr.
Your son had earlier been shot
    Where presently you were.

I'll call you our most brilliant man,
    And if they prove me wrong
I'll still insist that you will do
    Until *he* comes along!

MYSTERY LADY

This famous historical lady,
    Whose original surname was Smith,
Has a record unmatched in our annals —
    A good one to test people with.

She was born in the township of Weymouth
    But became, later on, a top resident
Of our capital city. The people
    Had elected her husband Vice-President.

She stayed in the capital city
    All through and beyond the four years
Which her husband then won in the White House —
    A strong, tactless leader, one hears.

Many things can be said of First Ladies,
    But *this* can be said of just one:
Her husband gained fame in the White House,
    Four Presidents later, her son.

NOTE: Who was she? Abigail Smith Adams (1744-1818) was the only woman whose immediate family included two Presidents of the United States — husband John Adams, our second President (1796-1800), and son John Quincy Adams, the sixth (1824-1828).

"JOHN PAUL JONES"

(John Paul, 1747-1792 A.D.)

John Paul? John Paul? Now, who was he?
    That name I do not know, sir.
Please tell me something of his life.
    Was he a friend or foe, sir?

You say he fought upon the sea
    Against the British warships?
I know of Lawrence, Perry, Hull —
    More men, and many more ships.

The Revolution, though, you say?
    That limits us severely.
John Barry, Whipple, Saltonstall —
    But Paul escapes me, clearly.

He got his ship in far-off France,
    An ancient tub, decaying?
He fought the brand-new *Serapis*?
    Do you know what you're saying?

This Captain Paul, was he the man
    Who battled half the night, sir?
Whose ship was sinking, yet who called,
    "I've just begun to fight!" sir?

Within the Navy chapel are
    His casket and his bones, sir?
That's not John Paul! The man you mean
    Is Captain J. P. Jones, sir!

What's that you say? His name's not Jones?
    That fact adds but to zero!
No matter what the name he bore
    He would have been a hero!

"MOLLY PITCHER"
(1754-1832 A.D.)

"Fetch your pitcher, Molly!
    Hurry, Molly! Run!
We need water, Molly!
    Water for the gun!"

On the field at Monmouth,
    Facing British red,
Fell your gunner-husband,
    Wounded — maybe dead.

Silent fell his cannon,
    None to wield the swab —
Silent, till you bravely
    Stepped into his job,

Wielding swab and rammer,
    Sponging out the bore,
Serving as a soldier,
    Helping win a war.

Till the charge was broken,
    You bestrode your man,
Fighting like a tigress!
    Then the tears began.

With the crisis over,
    Someone took the swab,
Handed you your pitcher,
    Gave you back your job.

"Fetch your pitcher, Molly!
    Hurry, Molly! Run!
We need water, Molly —
    Water for the gun!"

BENEDICT ARNOLD
(1741-1801 A.D.)

I'm puzzled, General, to know
    Just what my thoughts are of you.
Without you, we might not have won,
    And yet I *cannot* love you!

Heroically, you led our men
    Through horrible privation,
Then, wounded, fell before Quebec,
    The hero of our nation.

When back we reeled before the foe,
    A rabble wildly fleeing,
You saved our men from British hands,
    Preserved our force-in-being.

The fleet you launched on Lake Champlain
    Lived up to the occasion.
Although you lost, you kept the foe
    From mounting an invasion.

On Saratoga's rolling field,
    Burgoyne at last surrendered.
You won the fight. To Gen'ral Gates
    The British sword was tendered.

You did a lot to win the war.
    You should have had much glory.
Before it came, your new-wed wife
    Made you an ardent Tory.

At spying, treachery, deceit,
    You soon were subtly playing.
You tried to give West Point away,
    Your nation's trust betraying.

In British red, you served the cause
    Of which your wife had prattled.
The war you'd won could not be lost,
    No matter how you battled.

Without you, we might not have won,
    And yet I cannot love you.
I'm puzzled, General, to know
    Just *what* my thoughts are of you!

THE RIVALS —
JOHN ADAMS AND THOMAS JEFFERSON
(1735-1826; 1743-1826 A.D.)

Among our American leaders
   Two men soared as high as the birds —
John Adams, a bringer of action,
   Tom Jefferson, master of words.

While we struggled for freedom from Britain,
   Both helped our new nation arise.
Tom J. wrote the great Declaration.
   John A. got us help and allies.

Both men had a genuine feeling
   That America had to be strong.
In the methods they thought should be followed,
   Each thought that the other was wrong.

John A. wanted strength for the nation.
   Tom J. favored rights for the states.
Each developed a party and argued
   In brilliant and bitter debates.

Each man had a chance to put forward
    The things that he felt should be done.
Tom J. had two terms in the White House.
    John A. had already had one.

Tom doubled the size of our country
    When he bought Louisiana from France.
He didn't approve of his action
    But he couldn't pass up such a chance.

With the passing of years they grew closer,
    For with time any rivalry ends.
They developed a fine correspondence
    And gradually turned into friends.

On one thing, the two met agreement —
    On choosing the right day to die:
In the fiftieth year of our freedom,
    Of all dates, on the fourth of July!

NOTE: The complete listing of the accomplishments of these two men would be very long indeed. Jefferson felt that his three greatest were the writing of the Declaration of Independence and Virginia's law protecting religious freedom, and the founding of the University of Virginia.

BENJAMIN FRANKLIN
(1706-1790 A.D.)

"Benjamin Franklin! I've heard of that name —
   A writer who lives here in Philly.
He edits an almanac some folks think smart
   And others regard as just silly."

"You're mistaken, my friend. The Franklin *I* know
   Is famed as an excellent printer.
His press pours out pamphlets and posters and such
   Through summer, spring, autumn, and winter."

"A printer? A publisher, doubtless you mean.
   His paper is better than most, sir.
The weekly he edits will some day gain fame
   As *The Saturday Evening Post*, sir."

"Now, *I* should know Franklin far better than you.
   He spared me calamity dire.
His fire department was right on the job
   Last year when my house caught afire."

"You're *all* very wrong. *I* know Franklin well.
   I met him a year ago, when, sir,
He was founding a school that in due course of time
   Will become the renowned U. of Penn., sir."

"But Franklin's a scientist — one of the best —
   Not the things that you fellows are claiming.
He sent up a kite and drew lightning to earth
   All sparking and flashing and flaming."

"A scientist? Bah! He's a *postmaster*, friends —
   The first that our country has known, sir.
He's speeded the mail along his post roads
   And marked every mile with a stone, sir."

"You all have me puzzled. The Franklin *I* know
   Is in politics up to his shoulders.
Without his advising, our country would fall
   Like a landslide of circular boulders."

"But how can Ben Franklin at politics play
   When he's over the ocean, in Paris?
As a diplomat, he knows far better than most
   How to win, build good will, not embarrass."

"Don't be angry, you fellows, for *nobody's* wrong.
   All nine are remarkably right, sirs!
Ben Franklin's gained fame in a number of ways.
   Egad, but that fellow is bright, sirs!"

JAMES MADISON

(1753-1836 A.D.)

Somehow I think, James Madison,
    That you have been short-changed.
More credits should have come to you
    For things that you arranged.

You gave Virginia good laws
    And got her folks to heed 'em.
The best of all was one which gave
    Complete religious freedom.

When troubles came with England's King
    And feelings turned so sour,
You saw at once the crying need
    For a strong central power.

The war was won. The colonies
    From English rule were freed.
Thirteen weak states would not be good.
    A nation was our need.

A constitution must be framed.
    That was the thing to do!
Among the men who drew it up
    None gave as much as you.

To vote our Constitution in,
   You labored night and day,
Wrote pieces for *The Federalist*
   With Hamilton and Jay.

In Congress, where you served four terms,
   You won some great debates,
Insisting that some powers should
   Be turned back to the states.

The Presidency came to you
   In an unhappy year,
With England chucking 'round her weight,
   And war a thing to fear.

You staved it off as long as you
   Could find one reason more.
It was unfair that people spoke
   Of "Mister Mad'son's War."

Folks know of you, not well enough,
   But know you, nonetheless,
For all the things you did for them,
   You need a better "press"!

NOTE: Though James Madison, our fourth President, is often deservedly spoken of as "the Father of Our Constitution," he should be known for many other things as well. He served in a time of many outstanding men, and perhaps the competition was just a little too strong!

ELI WHITNEY

(1765-1825 A.D.)

When you went to Georgia,
   A boy fresh from Yale,
You hiked through the farmlands
   Across hill and dale.

You had never seen cotton
   A crop in the fields.
With such plantings, you wondered,
   Why not bigger yields?

The reason, they told you,
   Arose from the need
Of cleansing the fibers
   Of every last seed,

A slow job, and painful,
   Performed by the hands
Of numerous workers
   In hard-working bands.

You designed a machine
   For freeing the cotton.
The design wasn't good;
   The performance was rotten.

Defeated, despondent,
   You went out and sat
By the chicken-yard fence
   And saw there a cat.

He'd inserted his paw
    Through a hole in the fence.
He sat there and waited,
    Excited and tense.

A chick wandered close.
    The cat's claws were quick.
They snatched out some feathers.
    The fence saved the chick.

Right there was your answer!
    You rushed to begin
To build your new engine —
    The first "cotton gin."

It worked to perfection,
    By cleaning more cotton
Than dozens of workers
    Had hitherto gotten.

You made the South prosper
    By raising the yield
Of the great cash-crop, cotton,
    Brought fresh from the field.

Today we still marvel
    At what you could do —
Our two great inventors,
    The tomcat and you.

NOTE: Though the cotton gin was Eli Whitney's most important invention, he made little money from it because of the government's delay in issuing him a protective patent and because the machine was so simple that it was easy to copy. He did not exclaim, as jokers sometimes say, "Keep your cotton-picking fingers off my gin," but he would have been justified in doing so. His machine greatly increased the prosperity of the South by swelling the annual cotton crop to about 200 times its former value within ten years. Not many years later, Whitney made a considerable fortune by manufacturing muskets for the United States government.

THE WHISKY REBELLION
(1791-1794 A.D.)

Sing a song of sixpence,
    A demijohn of corn,
Hamilton will tax it,
    Sure as you are born.

When the tax was ordered
    The farmers booed and hissed,
Feathering the tax-men,
    Swearing to resist.

Have your fun, oh farmers!
    Utter yells and whoops.
Hamilton is coming,
    Leading in the troops.

Sing a song o' billions —
    Pattern for the nation.
Anything with profits
    Brings us new taxation.

JOHN JAMES AUDUBON
(1780-1851 A.D.)

A round peg in a square-shaped hole,
    A failure in all things —
You must acknowledge this was so
    (Except for things with wings.)

You failed to gain promotion in
    The naval school in France.
Though ships and battles bored you, birds
    Had power to entrance.

Your mill in Pennsylvania failed.
    You couldn't make it pay.
One cannot be a businessman
    While painting birds all day.

Then Lucy Bakewell shared your love,
    Part wife and two parts saint.
She worked to keep the wolf away,
    Permitting you to paint.

The bird life of America
    Your canvasses displayed —
The birds of prairie and of sea,
    Of forest and of glade.

Your book of colored prints of birds
    Intrigued, enchanted, thrilled.
Men came to know that birds were more
    Than something to be killed.

You spent your life depicting birds,
    Your passion to the end.
We hail you, J. J. Audubon —
    Of men and birds, the friend!

AARON BURR

(1756-1836 A.D.)

Oh, bright, erratic Mr. Burr,
    You should have traveled far.
Too bad you based your course upon
    A comet, not a star!

One cannot deal with slick intrigue
    And to the summit vault.
One eye looked up, the other down.
    That was your major fault.

You swore that it was Hamilton
    Who did your rise deter.
You killed him. You could never see
    Your greatest foe was Burr!

ANDREW JACKSON
(1767-1845 A.D.)

There was fire in your soul
And pepper, too.
You, a poor boy, orphaned early,
With little formal schooling,
Born in the South, then living in the West,
Daring to match your qualifications
Against those of the high-born Eastern aristocrats.
It was a miracle that you won out —
One of our nation's many miracles.

Let us look back:

We see you first in the Revolution,
A daring boy of thirteen years,
Joining a group of raiders
To attack a British column,
Failing, captured, and confined.
"No, sir! I will not black your boots!
I am your prisoner, not your slave!"
In time, the sword cuts made by the officer would heal
But the memory would not —
An expensive error by old Britain.

We see you next at twenty-one,
A lawyer now,
Leaving Carolina in a covered wagon,
Traveling westward into Tennessee,
Finding there your good wife Rachel,
Building with her your great house,
The Hermitage, in Nashville,
Where almost any visitor was welcome.

We note your shifting from the law to politics,
Serving briefly in both houses of Congress,
Opposing, always opposing, the ways of those
Who ran our government:
"The ordinary people of our country
Should have their say as well!"

War seemed to bring you out.
We see you in 1812,
In our second war with Britain
And her many Indian allies.
You are leading troops against the Creeks,
Defeating them at Horseshoe Bend,
Ending forever the menace of these western tribes.
Then you are invading Spanish Florida,
Taking Pensacola,
Hanging British agents who had sent the tribes
Against our southern states,
A move which later led our country
To purchase Florida from Spain.
Now we see your first great glory,
Defending New Orleans against a mighty British force,
Making the enemy lose two thousand men
While you were losing seventy-one.
Now, at last, the memory of those sword slashes
Could be forgotten.

The war over, and you a hero,
We watch you ride the crest of popularity
Toward the highest office in the land.
We admire the way you took your first defeat,
In 1824, by John Quincy Adams,
The thorough trouncing you gave him
The next time round, in '28,
And your victory over Henry Clay, in '32.
You loved the sweet smell
Of victory.

The Presidency, we learn, was not always the prize
It first had seemed.
We see you face a time of crises,
With your new views against the old:

We applaud your firm treatment of South Carolina
When she refused to obey
The high Tariff Law of 1832
Until you'd ordered in General Scott
And the army.
"The Federal Union, it must and shall be preserved."
That was your toast, and it saved the Union.

There's less approval of your treatment
Of Henry Clay's great national bank,
The Second Bank of the United States.
You hated and distrusted banks,
So you struck this one down,
Taking out the government's money,
Causing the bank to fail.
The result was a great depression
From which the country suffered.
Not all your acts were wise
And well considered.

Despite mistakes, we see our government live on,
Gaining in strength,
Giving encouraging proof
That an ordinary, honest man
Without superior education or aristocratic family
Can be an important President
Even in perilous times.

"Old Hickory" they called you,
For hickory wood is strong and tough —
Almost as strong and tough
As you had proved to be.

FRANCIS SCOTT KEY
(1779-1843 A.D.)

Francis Scott Key simply happened to be
   On a British warship, the *Surprise*.
He had gone to attend the release of a friend,
   When a battle broke out, 'fore his eyes.
The 1812 war had gone badly. What's more
   Our capital city'd been burned.
The great British fleet was intent to repeat
   Its success, and on Baltimore turned.
As the sun settled down, Key could make out the town
   With its forts very badly outgunned.
Through the dark of the night, fiercely raged the great fight,
   Cannonading that left a man stunned!
As the shooting died out, Key was left in grave doubt:
   Had the forts or the fleet won the fray?
Was our flag still on high? Did our men win or die?
   In the darkness of night, who could say?
With the first morning light, Key exclaimed with delight,
   For our flag on the fortress still flew.
The great British fleet had encountered defeat,
   And it presently turned and withdrew.

Key soon put into rhyme what he'd felt at the time,
    And his verse was read widely and soon.
Then, on everyone's tongue, it was joyfully sung
    To a popular music-hall tune.
It was in this manner *The Star Spangled Banner*
    Came to be, which our anthem supplies.
(Except that third verse. It's insulting, or worse,
    And the British are now our allies.)

NOTE: Francis Scott Key, a lawyer of Maryland and Washington, D.C., visited the British fleet under a flag of truce to secure the release of an American civilian, Dr. William Beanes. Instead of remaining aboard briefly, as he had intended, he was forced to remain with the fleet for eleven days, during which time the attack was made on Baltimore (night of September 13-14, 1814). After the battle, both Key and Dr. Beanes were released, Key bearing in his pocket the envelope on which he had written his poem about the attack. Friends to whom he showed the poem had copies struck off and widely spread. Ferdinand Durang, a musician-actor, fitted the words of Key's poem to the music of a then-popular song, "To Anacreon in Heaven," and first sang it while standing on a chair in a Baltimore tavern. The song quickly became popular throughout the United States, but it was not until 1931 that it was officially made our national anthem by act of Congress. Singers today usually sing the first, second, and fourth stanzas, omitting the bitter third one. The name of the composer of the music is unknown.

HENRY CLAY

(1777-1852 A.D.)

Hurray! Hurray!
For Henry Clay!

    The thing he wanted most in life
        Was never his to claim.
    His failure to be President,
        He felt, besmirched his name.
    Though three times picked to run the race,
        He lost out just the same.

    He had a brilliant law career
        But quit, his name to save.
    He never lost a murder case —
        Saved many from the grave.
    "I've freed too many who should hang,"
        Was the excuse he gave.

    When Britain seized our sailor men,
        "Impressing" for her fleet,
    The "war hawks," led by Henry Clay,
        The drums of war did beat.
    We fought and won, then Clay at Ghent
        Sat down, peace terms to treat.

When slavery split our land in twain,
    Those 'gainst it and those for,
Clay twice brought peace by compromise
    Before the guns could roar.
Had he lived on, we well might not
    Have had our Civil War.

Though he was never President,
    I think it safe to say
Few chief executives have used
    Their powers, in their day,
To help our land survive and grow,
    As well as Henry Clay.

That's why I say
"Hurray! Hurray!
For Henry Clay!"

DONALD McKAY

(1810-1880 A.D.)

White wings on the oceans,
      Clippers on the foam,
Cargoes bound for China,
      Tea ships rolling home.

In your yards in Boston,
      In your docks and slips,
Grew the graceful Clippers —
      Artistry in ships.

Rounded hulls for speeding,
      Masts to scrape the stars,
Sails to trap the breezes,
      Long and tapered spars,

Bows to cut the billows,
      Lines and names to please,
Flying Cloud and *Lightning*,
      Sovereign of the Seas,

Staghound, *Great Republic*,
      Heeling with the gale,
Footing fast, then faster,
      With their clouds of sail.

Where the sailors hearkened
      To the bosun's pipes,
Seamen knew your clippers,
      Knew the Stars and Stripes.

None could build their equals.
      None could match their speed.
Many tried to copy.
      No one could succeed.

From your yards and slipways,
      Out of Boston Bay,
Sailed your masterpieces,
      Artist Don McKay.

STEPHEN FOSTER

(1826-1864 A.D.)

Gentle Stephen Foster,
    Writer of our songs,
When we hear your music
    Ghosts arise in throngs —

Treasured ghosts — Susannah;
    Weeping, while we roam,
Loved ones long departed;
    Old Kentucky Home;

Lazy Swannee River;
    Mellow harvest moons;
Old Black Joe, a-dyin';
    Lively minstrel tunes;

Dashing Camptown Races;
    Voices hushed in prayer;
Tearful joys, recalling
    Jeannie's light-brown hair.

Some men fight our battles.
    Others right our wrongs.
Thank you, Stephen Foster,
    For those lovely songs.

STEPHEN DOUGLAS
(1813-1861 A.D.)

Ah, Stephen Douglas, you were great —
    A man earmarked for fame.
Your brilliant mind and nimble tongue
    Would elevate your name
Until at last, as sure as fate,
    You to the White House came.

You started out to make the climb.
    The bar you quickly gained,
The legislature, judgeship, too.
    The Senate you attained.
Now, looking upward, you could see
    One step alone remained.

"The Little Giant" you were called
    By followers compliant
Who thought to see you conquer all
    You met, who proved defiant.
Then, suddenly, your rise was stopped.
    You met a bigger giant!

It's no disgrace, Judge Douglas, sir,
    That Lincoln laid you low.
All students of the boxing ring
    Can quote a thing they know:
"A good *big* man can always beat
    A good, though smaller, foe."

ULYSSES S. GRANT AND ROBERT E. LEE

(1822-1885; 1807-1870 A.D.)

Two men more different seldom meet
   In ardent rivalry.
In normal times, in days of peace,
   It would be hard to see
What bond united these two men —
   The gen'rals Grant and Lee.

Except in war, Ulysses Grant
   Failed everything he tried.
In business, he could not succeed.
   In farming, his crops died.
But on the field of battle, he
   Just would not be denied.

Lee was a thorough gentleman.
   He was a scholar, too.
His mind was keen and orderly,
   The kind that thinks things through.
In peace or war, he seemed to be
   The better of the two.

Did Lee win out? No, it was Grant!
  He had more guns and men.
Despite great losses, he attacked
  Again! Again! Again!
He wore Lee's battered army out,
  And Lee surrendered then.

There were hard feelings in this war
  Of brother against brother.
Each leader, though, could understand
  The problems of the other.
Each craved to win, but Grant and Lee
  Respected one another.

NOTE: One can anticipate objection to the statement that "except in war, Ulysses Grant failed everything he tried." After all, he *was* elected President of the United States, wasn't he? He was indeed, but he was trusting and unsuspicious, and because of this many dishonest people gained government positions which they used to cheat the citizens. The Grant, Harding, and Nixon administrations are probably the three most bitterly criticized regimes in our history. His success as a general, though, was undeniable. Lincoln said it best. When a group of politicians sought the removal of General Grant, during the war, the President said, "I can't spare that man. He fights."

DAVID FARRAGUT

(1801-1870 A.D.)

Hail to the admiral,
    Showing the way,
Straight through the minefields
    Into Mobile Bay,
Shaming his captains,
    Scorning their dread,
"Damn the torpedoes!
    Full speed ahead!"

Think of the admiral
    In this new day.
Weapons and perils are
    Massed in our way.
"Yield to a conqueror?
    Better be dead!
Damn the torpedoes!
    Full speed ahead!"

ABRAHAM LINCOLN

(1809-1865 A.D.)

(A Sonnet)

Your unexpected climb to fame in life
   Was hindered by adversity and woes.
A man of peace, you had to deal with strife,
   As countrymen and friends became fierce foes.
With little education in your youth,
   You had to deal with problems deep and vast.
A homely, awkward man some called uncouth,
   You handled tasks undreamed of in the past —
To win a war, to free the slaves, to knit
   A riven country back to one again.
You had it almost done when you were hit;
   Booth's heavy bullet put you out of pain.
We know today the things that made you great:
Your mind, your soul, your heart devoid of hate.

THE GUN-SLINGERS

(c. 1875)

We are the rough and rugged men,
    The heroes of the West.
We're gunmen, all, of great renown;
    We're often called the best.
You know us — Dillon, Wyatt Earp,
    Bill Bonney, and the rest.

We ride the trails and rule the towns
    With fist and knife and gun.
All men who seek to challenge us
    Are quickly on the run.
With .44's that seldom miss,
    We kill them, every one.

But there's one group of supermen
    We never want to see.
We wouldn't have a chance with them.
    They'd shoot us down with glee.
They are the men who *never* miss,
    Who'll play us on TV!

STREET INCIDENT

(c. 1878)

One day on the street a young black man appeared,
    Back bowed, bearing two heavy bags.
With the greatest of effort he struggled along
    Through a series of tugs, lifts, and drags.

In time, he encountered another young man —
    A husky, athletic white boy.
"Here, friend, let me help you," the newcomer said.
    The black man accepted with joy.

As the two walked together, they chatted a bit,
    In the midst of their heavy-load hiking.
Each found in the other a genuine worth.
    They developed a mutual liking.

It's hard at the outset to look far ahead
    And see how an episode ends.
Neither boy could have told, as they struggled along,
    That they would become lasting friends.

"You have helped me a lot," the colored boy said.
    "Such help from a stranger is fine.
Booker T. Washington; that is my name."
    "And Theodore Roosevelt is mine."

ALEXANDER GRAHAM BELL
(1847-1922 A.D.)

Your contribution to the world
    Was vital, Mr. Bell,
But whether it was bad or good
    Is something I can't tell.

How shall we judge your great device?
    No one can doubt its use;
Conversely, almost everyone
    Deplores its wide abuse.

A child is sick. A call is made,
    And help is on the way.
A party-line subscriber blocks
    Your line for half a day.

A prowler lurks about your yard.
    You summon the police.
Wrong numbers tear you from your work.
    And cause your rest to cease.

Your daughter phones that she is well.
    It's good to hear her laugh.
A busybody calls and wastes
    An hour and a half.

A fire breaks out in the night.
    The engines come with speed.
A salesman calls and tries to sell
    You something you don't need.

The time that's saved means everything
    To people who are busy.
Teen-agers lie upon their spines
    And chatter 'til they're dizzy.

You started out to help the deaf
    And did so, it appears.
Yet you've afflicted millions more
    With ringing in the ears!

HENRY FORD
(1863-1947 A.D.)

"Put, a-put, a-putput!"
    The shop is full of smoke.
Henry's in there, working.
    (Working! That's a joke!)

"Put, a-put, a-putput!"
    What a fool he's been,
Fitting up a carriage
    With a gas machine!

"Put, a-put, a-putput!"
    Better get a horse!
If he starts out riding,
    He'll walk back, of course!

"Put, a-put, a-putput!"
    See the carriage run,
Scooting down the highway.
    Say! That looks like fun!

"Put, a-purr, a-purry!"
    Gee, how smooth that feels!
Henry, the mechanic,
    Put us all on wheels.

GEORGE WASHINGTON CARVER
(1864-1943 A.D.)

Few famous people catch the eye
   As young as sixty days,
But this young black was stolen then,
   A ransom fee to raise.

Night riders took the boy away —
   A hard and lawless crew —
Into a distant Southern state.
   They stole his mother, too.

The mother never could be found.
   She had been sold, of course.
The baby's owner bought him back.
   His ransom was a horse!

The Civil War came to an end,
   And small black George was free.
Since Kansas never had had slaves,
   'Twas there, at ten, went he.

He worked up through the high school grades
   Then took a college course
In Iowa, on growing plants —
   A freed slave's first resource.

From student to professor, he
    Advanced, for he had seen
The many things that can be done
    When mind is quick and keen.

He journeyed south to study at
    Tuskegeee Institute,
Where he could learn all man might know
    Of plants, from leaf to root.

From peanuts, he made wondrous things.
    From sweet potatoes, too —
A better cotton, marble, dyes,
    From plants that round him grew.

Among the things that he improved,
    Perfected, put to use,
Was his own race, the new-freed blacks,
    Arising from abuse.

He set a fine example which
    Could banish doubt and fear.
Few men have better proved their worth
    Than this black pioneer.

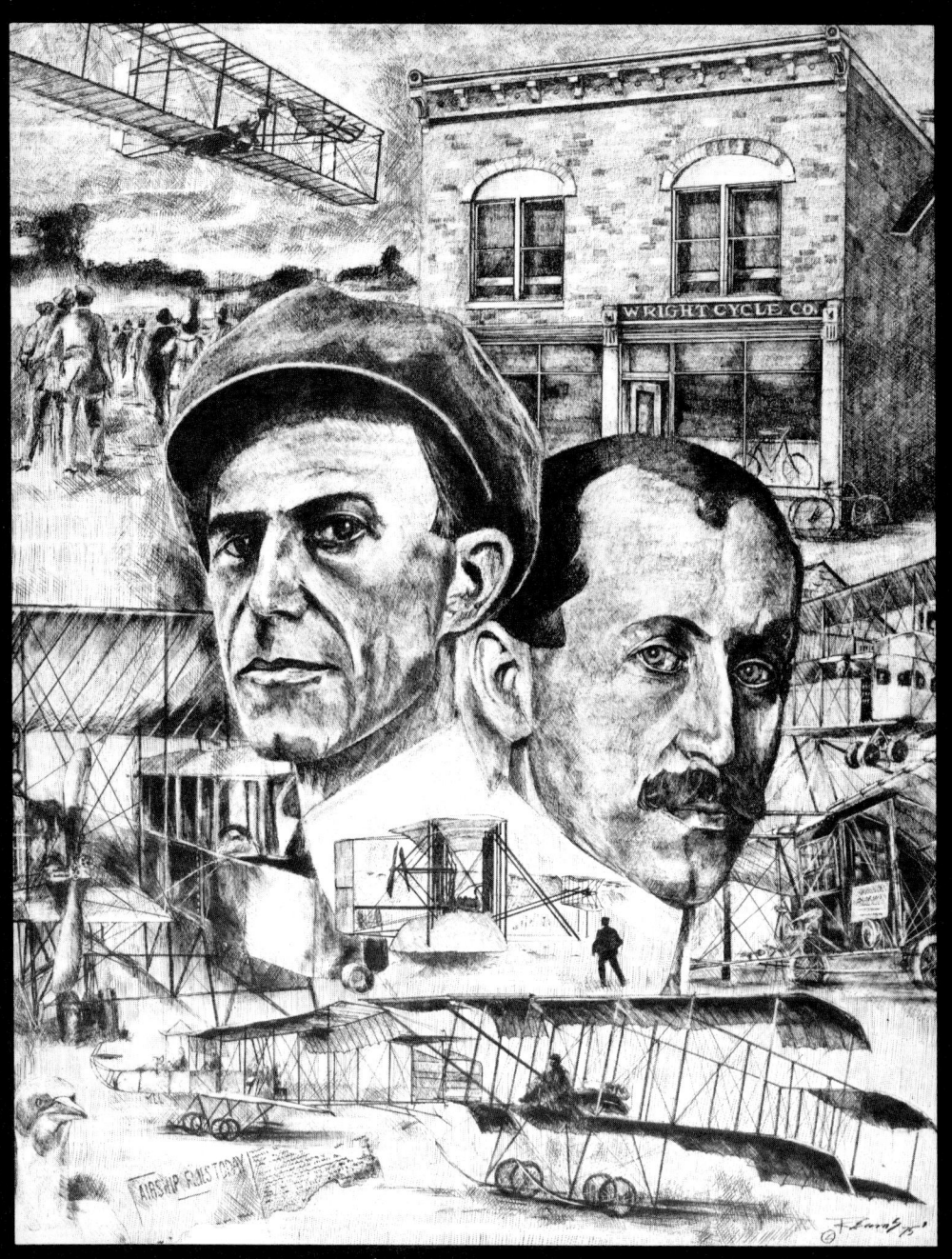

THE WRIGHT BROTHERS

(1867-1912; 1871-1948 A.D.)

The bike repair shop's closed and locked.
    The Wrights have gone away
To windy, sandy Kitty Hawk
    To waste their time in play —
To waste their time with giant kites
    A-soaring in the sky,
To try to prove to honest folks
    That men can learn to fly!

        They're stupid fools —
          Now, mark my words! —
        To think that men
          Can fly like birds!

The word is in. They've really flown!
    The thing took off and flew!
It carried Orville through the air;
    It carried Wilbur, too!
These two young men could see the way,
    They had the nerve to dare,
And man has left the earth to claim
    The kingdom of the air.

        I knew they could!
        I've always said
        The brothers Wright
          Would get ahead!

CARRY NATION
(1846-1911 A.D.)

"Mistress Carry, quite contrary,
    Tell me what you know."
"Demon Rum to town has come,
    And I'm his mortal foe."

"Mistress Carry, so contrary,
    How does the struggle go?"
"Mirrors crashed and bartops slashed
    And bottles smashed in a row."

"Carry! Carry, so contrary!
    What do you hope to do?"
"Before I die, my ax and I
    Will prove the Demon's through!"

THE SUFFRAGETTES

(1848-1920 A.D.)

To you, my dears, our hats are off.
    We must and do confess
That we were wrong denying you
    Your rights. (Gad! What a mess!)

It wasn't only votes, dear girls,
    That we, the men, withheld,
But rights *re* property and kids.
    (No wonder you rebelled!)

With leaders such as Susan A.,
    Lucy and Betty S.,
Julia Ward H. and Clara B.,
    You changed our "No!" to "Yes!"

It took a long and tough campaign
    Before our wall was cracked
And "Equal Rights for Womenkind!"
    Became a legal fact.

For women*kind* we can't regret
    What you have made us do,
Though we're unhappy at the thought
    The *unkind* got it too!

NOTE: The initialed ladies above were Susan B. Anthony, Lucy Stone, Elizabeth Cady Stanton, Julia Ward Howe, and Clara Barton, to whom we might well have added England's Emmaline Pankhurst, who fought the fight on both sides of the ocean.

PHINEAS T. BARNUM
(1810-1891 A.D.)

THE GREATEST SHOWMAN IN THE WORLD!
    That was your cherished label.
The things you did to foil the mob
    Outfabled any fable.

A well-shaved monkey drew a crowd.
    (You'd labeled it A FAIRY.)
An ordinary camel was
    THE PROPHET'S DROMEDARY.

GEORGE WASHINGTON'S NURSE turned out to be
    An old and kindly Negress.
To clear the crowd, you made a sign:
    THIS WAY TO REACH THE EGRESS.

Your farm at Bridgeport caught the eye
    Of many a commuter.
An elephant to draw a plow!
    (What ad was ever cuter?)

Your SWEDISH NIGHTINGALE, Miss Lind,
    Sang sweeter than a linnet,
Yet you're the very man who said,
    "There's one born every minute."

To see THE GREATEST SHOW ON EARTH,
    Folks rallied 'round quite gaily.
The circus brought much gold to you
    And just as much to Bailey.

It's strange nobody bore a grudge.
    I've pondered and concluded
As long as folks are entertained
    They *like* to be deluded!

MAN OF CONTRADICTIONS
(Theodore Roosevelt)
(1858-1919 A.D.)

He held many jobs, and did most of them well,
   His titles too numerous for us to tell,
But there is one truth which I feel free to state:
   Consistency wasn't his outstanding trait.
Bellicose! Warlike! A hard man to beat!
   He strengthened our land when he built up the fleet,
But the outfit he led was the strangest of forces,
   A cavalry unit that fought without horses.
Warlike you say! Such a bellicose man!
   Yet he *ended* a war twixt the Russ and Japan!
And received for his efforts, I hasten to tell,
   That greatest award — the Peace Prize, Nobel!
He also gained fame as "political mother" —
   Gave birth to one party, but won with another!
Great hunter! Explorer! He sought lasting fame
   By finding a river to carry his name,
But when the discussion had died to a shout
   The name that survived was "the River of Doubt."
This lover of action took time to compose
   A number of books in clear, eloquent prose.
What subject? All subjects! Scarce two were the same.
   They ranged from ideals to hunting big game.
Most people gain fame through but one skill, you know.
   T.R. was adept at a dozen or so.

NOTE: Theodore Roosevelt's "cavalry unit that fought without horses" was the famous Rough Riders, who charged on foot up San Juan Hill, during the Spanish-American War. The political party to which he "gave birth" was the Progressive Party, which unsuccessfully supported him for President in 1912, when a Democrat, Woodrow Wilson, was elected. Earlier, in 1900, the Republicans had elected Roosevelt Vice-President, and he had become President upon the death of William McKinley, in 1901. "The River of Doubt" *(Rio Duvida),* also sometimes called the *Rio Téodora* after Theodore Roosevelt, who claimed to have discovered it in 1914, is in northern Brazil.

VERMONT DOES NOT ANSWER
(1872-1933 A.D.)

The owl's known for wisdom great
    And so was Calvin C.
The reason for this parallel
    For years eluded me.
I've pondered it, and now I think
    I've stumbled on the key.

    Cal Coolidge and the big-eyed bird
    Just sat and stared, without a word.

You might have thought it was a tie
    Between the bird and man —
A dead heat by the stillest pair
    Since life on earth began.
It was, at first, but Coolidge won,
    As humans often can.

    The owl queried "Who?" at last.
    But Calvin kept his lips shut fast.

LEE DE FOREST

(1873-1961 A.D.)

When you produced the audion
    And sound flew without wire,
Were you convinced you'd done much good
    Or were your feelings dire?

Did you regard the radio
    As spreading needed news,
Or did commercials come to mind
    Of toothpaste, lipstick, shoes?

Was education in your mind,
    Improving mental powers,
Or did you of soap operas think
    To waste the housewife's hours?

Your radio has brought a host
    Of good things and of bad.
It's complicated very much
    The simple life we had.

Did you not feel a glow of pride
    At all this great upheaval?
Or did you mean it when you punned
    "This is De Forest's prime evil"?

GRANDMA MOSES

(1860-1961 A.D.)

(Written in 1960)

Over the river and through the woods,
    To Grandmother's house we go.
This isn't the usual Christmas drive
    By sleigh, on the winter snow.
We're going to buy a work of art
    From a painter whom we know.

Though Grandma Moses is not our kin,
    We feel that we know her well.
She paints the beauty we've often seen —
    The farm in the country dell,
The fields of green, the barns of red,
    The homes where the farm-folks dwell.

For seventy years, as a farmer's wife,
    She devoted her life to toil,
Working to wring a living hard
    From the unforgiving soil.
When most of us feel that life is through,
    She started to paint in oil.

Now thirty years of art she's known,
    And her century's gone full-turn.
We share her joy at the heart-felt praise
    Her country pictures earn.
She has lived two lives, and each contains
    Lessons we all should learn.

FRANKLIN DELANO ROOSEVELT
(1882-1945 A.D.)

Too bad, young man! At thirty-nine,
    Your fate has been decreed,
Your legs struck numb with polio.
    Now you can never lead.
We'll write you off and soon forget
    The promise you have shown.
Man cannot rise above such blows.
    This, Man has always known.

What word is this? You've carried on
    And govern now the state.
Incredible! It can't be true!
    We won't have long to wait
To see you fail. Ah, here's the word!
    You're *President*, no less!
You've overreached this time, my friend.
    Things will go hard, I guess.

Your only hope as President
    Is that the times be good.
If not, you'll never stand the gaff.
    You'll fail. I said you would.
The times *aren't* good. Depression's here,
    And here come foreign foes —
The Nazis, Fascists, Japanese —
    The Good Lord only knows

What they will do, these warlike ones,
    What you can do in turn.
You cannot win! I'm asking you:
    When *will* you ever learn?
The war goes on. You're *winning* now!
    The odds meant not a thing.
I don't know how, but you have licked
    Whatever Fate could bring.

While you contended, you have set
    Another record more —
The only President to win
    Not two terms, three, but four!
And now you're gone, I must confess
    How very wrong I've been.
It's not a man's outside that counts,
    But what he has within!

PARKER BUCK
— NEIGHBORHOOD HERO
(1898-1918 A.D.)

When off to war you gaily went
    In 1917,
To meet the Germans in the sky,
    Machine against machine,
We younger boys were deeply thrilled
    To know a man like you.
Our dearest wish was that we could
    Do what we knew you'd do.

From time to time, your brother gave
    Us tidings of your life.
A flying field in Texas
    Was preparing you for strife.
The airborne combat still would come
    When you went overseas.
'Twas then the final message came
    That caused our blood to freeze:

Your plane had crashed upon the field,
    In Texas, not in France.
You'd fallen free, uninjured,
    Through amazing, lucky chance.
Your crewman, though, was trapped within
    The shattered, burning plane.
You staggered up, then sprinted back
    Into the flames again.

'Twas not to be. You could not save
    Your crewman's menaced life.
You both met death within the plane
    From fire — not from strife.
No lasting fame has come to you
    From sacrifice so grim,
But if a greater hero flew
    I have not heard of him.

RALPH BUNCHE, PIONEER
(1904-1971 A.D.)

When you set out, Ralph Johnson Bunche,
   To fashion your career,
Your aim was high and never low.
   You showed no doubt or fear.

The greatest schools and colleges
   Proved not beyond your reach.
You showed your skill at study there
   And, later, skill to teach.

When World War II came roaring in,
   You proved that you were great,
First in Strategic Services
   Then in the Halls of State.

The war was won, but you kept on
   Achieving lofty stations,
With various positions in
   The great United Nations.

Count Bernadotte was dying then,
   So you served in his lieu,
Achieving peace in Palestine
   For Arab and for Jew.

As just reward you then received
    The Nobel Prize for Peace,
Then carried on your blessed work
    Of causing wars to cease.

Eternal peace is hard to get.
    Old quarrels seethe and boil.
It needs eternal vigilance
    And everlasting toil.

Now you are gone, but you have shown
    The way it can be done —
A peaceful route, dependent on
    The treaty, not the gun.

The others who come seeking peace
    Will look to you for aid.
They'll follow, thankfully, your path,
    The footprints you have made.

All hail to you, Ralph Johnson Bunche!
    Our debt to you is vast —
First of your race to reach so high,
    The first, but not the last!

"WE" —
CHARLES AUGUSTUS LINDBERGH
(1902-1974 A.D.)

You came out of nowhere and thrilled us —
    First flier to conquer the sea
Alone in a single-hop journey —
    Alone, though you told it as "we."

At first this strange term posed a riddle.
    As they pondered it over again
Your listeners reached the conclusion
    That by "we" you meant you and your plane.

Later on, when you'd married Anne Morrow
    And she shared in your flights and your life,
It seemed that your "we" had expanded
    To include you, your plane, and your wife.

To your flying was added med. science
    When you helped Doctor Carrel to build
A life-saving pump. "We" included
    This man, humanistic and skilled.

With the birth of your young came expansion,
    Though your "we" was constructed in grief
When your first little boy was abducted
    And killed by a kidnaping thief.

Now you've gone, but you've left with the people
    A conviction 'twould be hard to lose:
That your "we" will be noted for greatness
    No matter which "we group" we choose.

TO A U.N. SOLDIER
DEAD IN A DISTANT LAND

Now you are dead —
Dead ere you reached your prime,
Dead in a foreign field,
Dead from the bullet of a man
You never knew
And never saw.

Why?

Did you wonder why
During those unreal moments
When your life was slipping out?
Did the thought intrude
Between the terror and the pain?

Now that you cannot ask,
We ask for you —
Why?

It can make no difference now to you,
But it does to us who live —
To all who are now alive.

Let us remember:

The armed services took you,
Plucked you from your chosen life,
Dressed you in a uniform,
Taught you how to fight,
To kill,
And sent you far away
To a strange land of which you'd hardly heard,
To serve under a strange flag —
A pale blue flag
With white laurel leaves
And a pure white globe.
It was not your nation's flag,
Yet you died for it.

Why?

Why did you fight so well
And give so much
To serve this strange new flag?
Why did you die
To save a land of strangers
From the aggressor?

Was it all in vain?

Perhaps you wondered,
Asked yourself,
Even at the end.

No, we can tell you,
It was not in vain.
For, when the years have passed
And the perspective sharpened,
Men will look back
Proudly,
Deeply moved,
And will mark well this turning
In the life of man.

"Here," they will say,
"Here, first of all,
Men stood together,
Free men,
Lovers of liberty,
And gave their lives
In defense of freedom.
Not *their* freedom, mark you,
But abstract freedom,
The freedom of a helpless people,
Menaced,
Invaded,
Determined to be free.
Here,
In this time,
In this place,
Was the turning point —
The guarantee of freedom,
Everywhere,
Forever,"

So they will say,
The breath catching in their throats,
Their hearts deeply stirred within them.

You had a part in this.
Your sacrifice was accepted.

A century from now,
When all of us have gone
As all men must —
Some nobly,
Some meanly —
This thing can be adjudged.

God grant this hundred years will see
The end of war,
The finish of aggression,
The triumph of the free,
The universal dignity of Man.

If so, who can deny
You played a vital part?

God grant it comes!

If not, what then?
What of your sacrifice —
Your death so far from home,
From all that you have known?
Will it then be in vain?

Can it be so
When for your epitaph you've earned the words,
The blessed words:
"Greater love hath no man than this,
That he give up his life
For his friend"?

Who would not trade epitaphs
With you?

NOTE: The above piece, I have learned to my pleasure, was read aloud to the United States delegation at the United Nations by Ambassador Henry Cabot Lodge.

J.V.D.S.

PRESIDENTIAL JINX

The President, each twenty years,
   Goes early to his bier.
Six Presidents the jinx has claimed.
   Now 1960's here!

In 1840, Harrison
   Won out (". . . and Tyler, too!")
Within a month, he sickened, and
   Quite quickly, he was through.

In 1860, Honest Abe
   Prevailed, then won again.
Booth's pistol bullet robbed us of
   One of our greatest men.

In 1880, Garfield won.
   A "dark horse" choice was he.
He turned an officer-seeker down.
   A bullet was his fee!

McKinley won in "oughty-ought."
   He'd had one term before.
A pistol-wielding anarchist
   Made sure he'd run no more.

In '20, it was Warren G.
    Who won the deadly prize.
He sickened on a western trip
    And met a quick demise.

In 1940, F.D.R.
    A third election tried.
He won again in '44,
    Then very quickly died.

The President, each twenty years,
    Goes early to his bier.
Six Presidents the jinx has claimed.
    Now 1960's here!

NOTE: This macabre prediction was written in the summer of 1960, before John F. Kennedy had even been nominated. Since 1840, the President elected each twenty years has died while still in office, though not always during the term starting with the jinx year. Only one other President, Zachary Taylor, has ever died in office. His death completes another jinx, that all Whig Presidents elected to office died within a year. Two Presidents, Lincoln and Kennedy, were shot through the head. Each was succeeded by a Vice President named Johnson.

    The editors of *Grit* Magazine felt it better not to publish this poem in their series because "it sounds as though you were predicting the death in office of our next President." That is precisely what I was doing. Now, how about 1980?

THE UNKNOWN FUTURE

We stand in the present
    In hope and in dread.
We know what's behind us
    But not what's ahead.

Our Earth's been explored.
    Now we look to the stars.
We've walked on the moon.
    Next on Venus and Mars?

A marvelous future?
    It might well be so,
But if we aren't wary
    Most likely it's "No!"

Some unfortunate evils
    Are starting to climb.
Must we suffer this upturn
    Of violence and crime?

Two "wars to end warfare"
    Have lately occurred.
No peace was forthcoming.
    Must there be a third?

Has the magic of science
    Been blessing or hex?
Has living improved
    Or just grown more complex?

The strife between sexes
    Is showing strong growth.
Too bad! There's no future
    For us without both.

There are rivalries grim
    Between nations and races,
Religions and parties
    And colors of faces.

Man's far from perfection.
    He quarrels and fights,
Neglecting his duties,
    Demanding his rights.

Cannot men come to see
    That they're really alike?
Can't their hands be extended
    To aid — not to strike?

In this perilous future
    Who'll save us? Who *can*?
If he puts his mind to it,
    This creature called *MAN*.

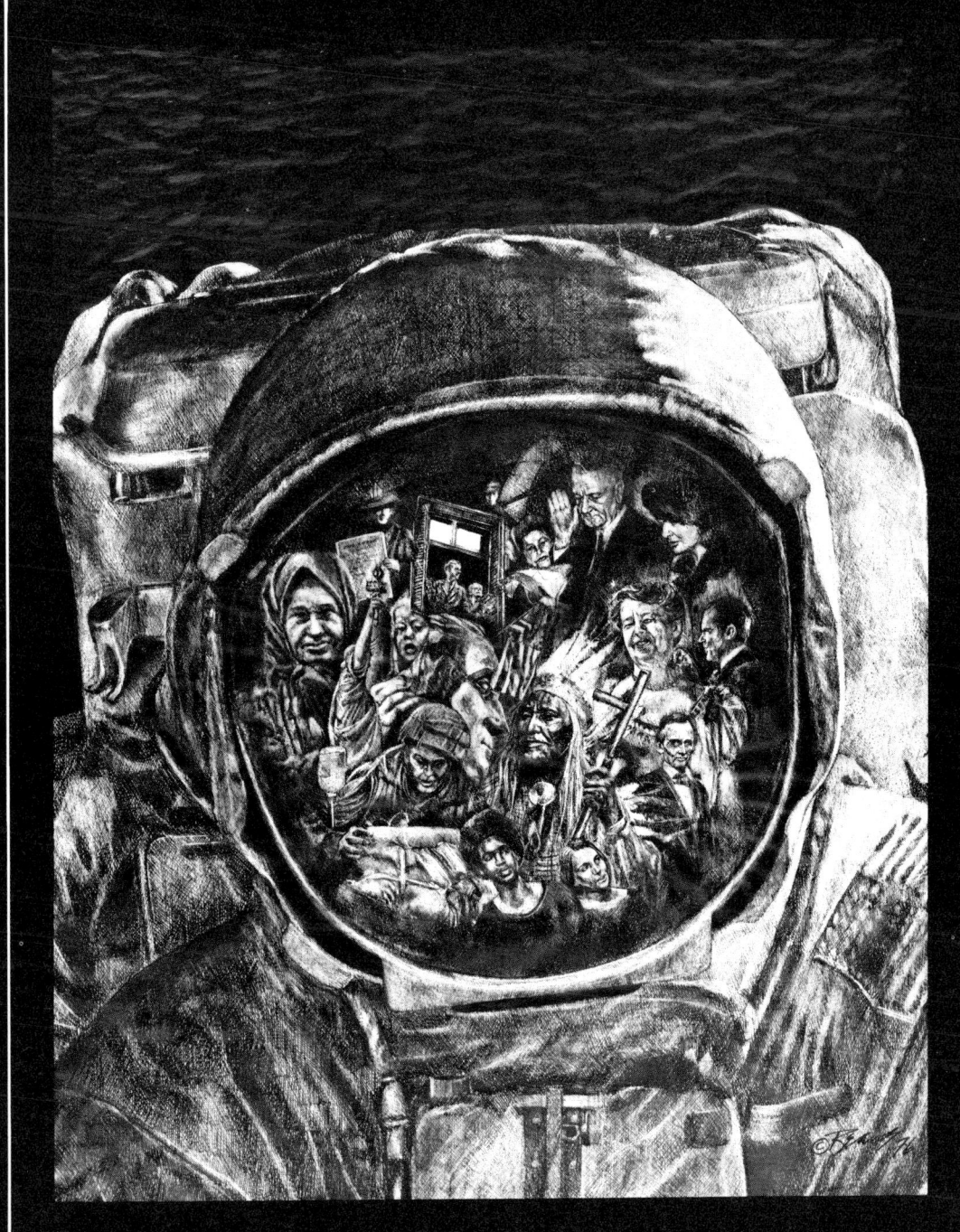

INDEX

Names and events mentioned in the verses or notes are indicated in Roman type; illustrations are indicated by Italic type, in parentheses.

Adams, Abigail Smith, 45
Adams, John, 33, 45, 52-53
Adams, John Quincy, 45, 66
Adams, Samuel, 33
Airplane, the, 91, *(90)*
Anthony, Susan B., 93
Arabs, 105
Arnold, Benedict, 50-51
Articles of Confederation, 43
Audubon, John James, 63, *(62)*

Bailey, J. A., 95
Bakewell, Lucy, 63
Baltimore, Md., 69
Barnum, Phineas T., 95, *(94)*
Barry, John, 47
Bartlett, Josiah, 33
Barton, Clara, 93
Beanes, Dr. William, 70
Bell, Alexander Graham, 84-85
Bernadotte, Count, 105
Bill of Rights, 36, 37
Bonney, Bill, 83
Boone, Daniel, 41
Booth, John Wilkes, 81, 113
Boston, Mass., 25, 73, 74
Braxton, Carter, 33
Bridgeport, Ct., 95
Brutus, Marcus Junius, 35
Buck, Parker, 103
Bunch, Ralph Johnson, 105-106, *(104)*
Burgoyne, General John, 50
Burr, Aaron, 44, 64

Caesar, Gaius Julius, 35
Cambridge, Mass., 21
Canonicus, 20
Carolina, 65
Carrel, Dr. Alexis, 107
Carroll, Charles, 33
Carver, George Washington, 88-89
Catholics, 22, 23
Champlain, Lake, 50
Charles I, King, 35
Chase, Samuel, 33
China, 73
Civil War, the, 72, 88
Clark, Abraham, 33

Clay, Henry, 66, 67, 71-72
Clipper ships, 73-74
Clymer, George, 33
Columbus, Christopher, 16
Common Sense, 38
Congress, 32, 33, 58, 66
Constitution, U.S., 36-37, 57
Coolidge, Calvin, 97
Cotton gin, the, 59-60
Creek Indians, 66
Crisis, the, 38
Cromwell, Oliver, 35

Dawes, William, 27, *(26)*
Declaration of Independence, 32-33, 52
Declaratory Act, 36
De Forest, Lee, 98
Dillon, Jack, 83
Douglas, Stephen A., 76
Durang, Ferdinand, 70

Earp, Wyatt, 83
Ellery, William, 33

Farragut, Admiral David G., 79
Fascists, 101
Federalist, the, 43, 57
Flag, American, 31, *(30)*
Florida, 66
Floyd, William, 33
Flying Cloud, the, 73
Ford, Henry, 87, *(86)*
Foster, Stephen Collins, 75
France, 23, 39, 47, 63, 103
Franklin, Benjamin, 33, 39, 55-56, *(54)*
Future, the Unknown, 115-116, *(117)*

Garfield, James A., 113
Gates, General Horatio, 50
George III, King, 33, 35, 36, 41, 43, 57
Georgia, 59
Gerry, Elbridge, 33
Ghent, Treaty of, 71
Grant, Ulysses S., 77-78
Great Britain, 29, 37, 38, 40, 49, 52, 65, 71, 116
Great Republic, the, 74
Gun-slingers, 83
Gwinnett, Button, 33

Hall, Lyman, 33
Hamilton, Alexander, 43-44, 61, 64, (42)
Hancock, John, 33
Harding, Warren G., 78, 113
Harrison, Benjamin, 33
Harrison, William Henry, 113
Hart, John, 33
Harvard, John, 21
Harvard University, 21
Henry, Patrick, 35-37, (34)
Heretics, 22
Hermitage, 65
Hewes, Joseph, 33
Heyward, Thomas Jr., 33
Hooper, William, 33
Hopkins, Stephen, 33
Hopkinson, Francis, 33
Horseshoe Bend, 66
House of Burgesses, 35
Howe, Julia Ward, 93
Hull, Captain Isaac, 47
Huntington, Samuel, 33

Indians, 15, 18-20, 40, (14)
Iowa, 88

Jackson, Andrew, 65-67
James I, King, 17
Japan, 96, 101
Jefferson, Thomas, 33, 52-53
Jesuits, 23
Jews (Israelis), 105
Jogues, Isaac, 23
Johnson, Andrew, 114
Johnson, Lyndon B., 114, (112)
Jones, John Paul, 47, (46)

Kansas, 88
Kennedy, John F., 114, (112)
Kentucky, 41
Key, Francis Scott, 69-70, (68)
Kitty Hawk, N.C., 91

Lalande, Jean, 23
Lawrence, Capt. James, 47
Lee, Francis Lightfoot, 33
Lee, Richard Henry, 33
Lee, Robert E., 77-78
Lewis, Francis, 33
Lightning, the, 73
Lincoln, Abraham, 76, 81, 113, (80)
Lind, Jenny, 95
Lindbergh, Charles A., 107
Livingston, Philip, 33
Lodge, Henry Cabot, 111

Louisiana, 53
Lynch, Thomas Jr., 33

Madison, James, 57-58
Mars, 115
Maryland, 70
Massachusetts, 22
Massachusetts Bay Colony, 21
Massasoit, 19
Mather, Cotton, 22
McKay, Donald, 73-74
McKean, Thomas, 33
McKinley, William, 96, 113
Middleton, Arthur, 33
Missouri, 41
Mobile Bay, 79
Mohawks, 23
Monmouth, N.J., 49
Moon, the, 115
Morris, Lewis, 33
Morris, Robert, 33
Morrow, Anne, 107
Morton, John, 33
Moses, "Grandma," 99
"Mother Goose," 25, (24)

Nashville, Tenn., 65
Nation, Carry, 92
National Bank, 67
Nazis, 101
Nelson, Thomas Jr., 33
Nevis, 43
New Orleans, La., 66
Nixon, Richard M., 78
Nobel Peace Prize, 96, 106

Paca, William, 33
Paine, Robert Treat, 33
Paine, Thomas, 38-39
Palestine, 105
Pankhurst, Emmaline, 93
Paris, 56
Parliament, 35
Paul, John, 47, (46)
Penn, John, 33
Pennsylvania, 63
Pennsylvania, University of, 55
Pensacola, Fla., 66
Perry, Oliver Hazard, 47
Philadelphia, Pa., ("Quaker Town"), 31, 55
Pilgrims, 17, 18
Pitcher, Molly, 49, (48)
Plymouth, Mass., 18, 20
Pope, the, 23
Prescott, Samuel, 27, (26)

Princeton, N.J., 29
Puritans, 22

Quebec, 50

Read, George, 33
Revere, Paul, 27, (*26*)
Revolution, American, 29, 37, 38, 40, 49, 50-51, 52, 65, (*26, 28, 46, 48*)
Rodney, Caesar, 33
Roosevelt, Franklin D., 101-102, 114, (*100*)
Roosevelt, Theodore, 82, 96
Ross, Betsy, 31, (*30*)
Ross, George, 33
Rush, Benjamin, 33
Russia, 96
Rutledge, Edward, 33

Saltonstall, Capt. Dudley, 47
Samoset, 18
Saratoga, N.Y., 50
Saturday Evening Post, the, 55
Scott, Gen. Winfield, 67
Serapis, the, 47, (*46*)
Sherman, Roger, 33
Slavery, 72
Smith, James, 33
South Carolina, 67
Sovereign of the Seas, the, 73
Spain, 16
Squanto, 19
Staghound, the, 74
Stamp Act, 35
Standish, Miles, 20
Stanton, Elizabeth Cady, 93
Star Spangled Banner, the, 69
Stockton, Richard, 33
Stone, Lucy, 93
Stone, Thomas, 33
Stony Point, Fort, 40
Suffragettes, 93
Surprise, the, 69

Tariff Law, 67
Taylor, George, 33

Taylor, Zachary, 113
Telephone, the, 84-85
Tennessee, 65
Texas, 103
Thornton, Matthew, 33
"To Anacreon in Heaven," 70
Torquemada, 22
Trenton, N.J., 29
Tuskegee Institute, 89
Tyler, John, 113

United Nations, 105, 108-111

Venus, 115
Vergoose, Elizabeth, 25, (*24*)
Vermont, 97
Virginia, 35, 36, 57
Virginia, University of, 53

Walton, George, 33
"War Hawks," 71
War of 1812, 66, 69
Washington, Booker T., 82
Washington, D.C., 70
Washington, George, 29, 39, 43, 44, (*28*)
Wayne, "Mad Anthony," 40
"We," 107
Weems, Parson, 29
West Point, 51
Weymouth, Mass., 45
Whipple, Capt. Abraham, 47
Whipple, William, 33
Whisky Rebellion, 61
White House, 45, 76
Whitney, Eli, 59-60
Williams, William, 33
Wilson, James, 33
Witherspoon, John, 33
Wolcott, Oliver, 33
World War I, 103
World War II, 102, 105
Wright, Orville, 91, (*90*)
Wright, Wilbur, 91, (*90*)
Wythe, George, 33

Yale University, 59